something
at the
window
is
scratching

something at the window is scratching

DEDICATED TO BOMB AND DAD

"This stuff just comes to you, huh?"
-My Dad

fOreward
by jhonen vasquez

Think back. No, farther back than that. No, even farther than that. NO, are you..

Look, if you're not even going to try, then just forget it, okay? I hate you, I'm leaving.

Wait, let's try again, yes? Do you remember being small? Can you remember being a disturbed little child? It's not as strange as it sounds to refer to kids, the proper ones anyhow, as disturbed. Nothing's as strange as it sounds.

We expect so much from people by the time they have "grown up", so much stability and so much...adulthood. You put a child's soul, symbol of purity, innocence and hope, into a grownup's body, and you would have what Earthling society would call a lunatic. The world would lock them away and wonder what went wrong with this unfortunate person, while forever lamenting their own loss of the very qualities the interpret as improper in the prisoner. Now I know what you're thinking, you're thinking, "So, exactly HOW do you extract a child's soul from its body? And by what device do you insert it into the body of a grownup? And what happened to the grownup's soul, seeing as how the body is empty when it receives the child's soul? Or is it NOT empty, but just pushed back to make room for the child's soul, just stuffed back in the darkest reaches of the body (perhaps the large intestine) screaming, SCREAMING to be released! Does anybody hear the screaming? I'm scared." Well the answer is simple.

But I won't get into that.

It's a lovely thing, and an evil pain in the ass to be the proud owner of such a soul. Lovely, because things like this book make sense, and provoke a smile, a distant sense of warmth in knowing that other brains are churning out the sort of beautiful nonsense that actually touches something in you retained from when you were so much smaller. Smaller and not a prisoner of expectation. It's a painful thing because you can see other people losing those qualities as they grow with you. You can watch as they shed off childhood like a skin they feel no longer suits them, emerging from this metamorphosis as a beautifully majestic specimen of the mundane.

These miserable clothed monkeys aren't the prisoner's

though, as a prison needs to contain something alive, something that knows there is more out there to be had.

Okay, I'm going to interrupt myself here and tell you that even I don't know where the hell I'm going with this thing. I'm not sure if it was supposed to be about how losing ones' own ability to love the absurd is a horrible thing, or if I was trying to divulge the secrets to some ghoulish government plan to rip the souls from children so that they could learn more about that sort of thing. All I really know now is that kids have a quality about them that lets them be insane, and gives them a playful lunacy that, quite simply, kicks ass. To successfully hold on to that quality and add it to things learned while and upon growing up is something akin to a super weapon against reality. To be able to revel in disgusting tales, and stories about monsters, and pear headed mutants whose friends get eaten by birds. To crack smiles, and laugh, and then honestly wonder how his bread-headed friend could have made it this long without having been eaten by birds longer ago.

I remember hearing stories like Red Riding Hood, and thinking with such focus on how it must have felt to be inside that wolve's stomach, and what it would have smelled like. I would try to imagine where the monsters in all of these classic stories came from, and how they lived before the stories began. Sometimes it's the lack of details that makes the story so everlasting. And it's the same here, In Roman Dirge's little book, as I ask myself, " What the hell is up with the sandman? I mean he can't fly? What's his problem that he actually steps into a bear trap?" I imagine he was distracted by something, and just had a lapse of attention. Also, his little son's ass freaks me out. These little details that are no more but implied, save perhaps for that eerie little butt-thing, are what make stories like these stick in my mind, and the minds of all the other kids out there who find they're alive in a world of the people who grew up and lost that special something, who grew up to be dead.

Okay, this thing ended up sounding so much more dreary than i had intended, but I got a semblance of a point across (Not an easy task at times), and I think that point is clear to anyone who was actually paying attention:

Children are criminally insane and must be destroyed.

Jhonen Vasquez

table of contents

the coo coo lady

There once was a lady
who loved her coo coo.
She sat in bed waiting—
that's all she would do.
Anxiously waiting
for that bird to appear,
knowing that soon
the time would be near.

Twice a day at twelve
the bird would come out.
"I love you dear birdie!"
the coo coo lady
would shout.

After 70 years
of coo coo—ing
the bird would

coo coo no more.
Horrified—
the coo coo lady lost
all that she had lived for.

Quickly,
the coo coo lady fell over—
dead from a broken heart.
She and her birdie
left this world
only six seconds apart.

critter pie

A little horror,
A scream, a cry...
That's how you make a critter pie.
They beg.
They plead.
They try to run.
This makes cooking so much fun.
Four to five critters would be nice.
The "big-boned" ones just add spice.
Everything must someday die—
might as well make a critter pie.

17

the sideways man

Long ago lived a vampire
who's body was crooked
on just one side.
He liked to take pictures
of all his victims
as they died.

He toured with a carnival
that traveled coast to coast,
bragging to his vampire friends
that he had killed the most.

The Sideways man heard a rumor
that there was another blood drinker in town.
So he went on a search,
destined to have
a vampire showdown.

It didn't take long
to find the foe that he sought.
He expected many things,
but this he did not.
Walking his direction
in the nite dim,
The Sideways Man's
long lost brother Ragamuffin
now stood before him.

"Hello dear brother!"
Ragamuffin spoke out.
"I knew this day would come.
Let us fight our final bout."
"No No," responded the Sideways Man.
"This is not how I want it to end.
I feel only love for you, my sibling.
Please just be my friend."

"You bragged that you're
the greatest killer.
You know that it's not true.
Your lie has been heard
by many.
Now there is only
one thing we can do."
With those last words,
the brothers clashed
into an epic fight.
They both fought bravely,
but only Ragamuffin walked away.
The Sideways Man lost the fight.

something
at the
window
is
scratching

A cold December night
as the snow comes down,
sleeping am I—
snug, quiet, not a sound.

I had long been visited
by Mr. Sandman—
away he took me
to Sleepytime Land.

I dream of
Ghosts, Goblins, and other creepy things,
feeling the fear
a dream like this brings.

And then suddenly,
as the egg of fear in me
is hatching,
I realize
that something at the window
is scratching.

Straight up sat I
with my eyes intent.
Watching the window
and what it will vent.
A dark pane of glass
is all that I see,
but I know that I heard it.
What could it be?

I ventured over to the window
and what should I see?
But an odd little creature
looking back at me.
Sanity left me
and my fear quickly followed suit,
as I felt that this being
was indeed harmless and cute.

Then the thing spoke
in an eerie little voice.
He was sorry to wake me,
but he hadn't a choice.
"I'm sorry," said he, "to give you such a fright,
but I'm looking for my daddy.
He did not come home this nite."
"You were the last one on his list," the creature did weep.
"I know that he's been here,
since I found you asleep."

I did not understand
the logic in what he had said.
My visitor knew his dad had been here
cause he found me in bed.
Just then I noticed
some footsteps out in the snow.
I jumped out the window
and away we did go.

We hadn't walked far
before we found something
very sad.
There in the snow,
was this poor orphan's dad.
It all made sense now
what the little monster had said.
The Sandman was his daddy
and now he was dead.
After he had left me from making me nap,
he froze to death,
caught in an old bear trap.

"No! No! No!"
the little Sandman began crying.
I told him it would be ok,
but he knew I was lying.
"I'm so alone in this world.
Who will take care of me and how?"
I thought for a second and said,
"You can live with me now."
"You would have to keep me a secret and I don't think
that you can."
"Trust me," said I.
"Tomorrow you will see my little plan."

The very next morning
I put my plan into action.
Tricking my parents
would be a very hard faction.
As around the breakfast table
we all sat,
I said, "Mom and Dad....
Meet our new cat."

UM...
MEOW?

mr- seephis

Poor Mr. Seephis
king of the bear people,
wearing a self—proclaimed crown
atop a homemade steeple.
All you want are bears to care about you—
warm, furry and kind.
Except for BoBo the killer bear
who was not so inclined.

little
lisa
loverbumps

Little Lisa Loverbumps
was the closest girl to me.
Until one day without warning
she walked out into the sea.

At first I thought she was joking—
funniest thing I'd seen all day—
but the joke was quickly over
as I watched her float away.

peter
the
pirate squid

There's not a whole lot he did—
Peter, the pirate squid.

the ghOst
in the spider

There once was a spider
with a ghost inside her—
and what a happy ghost it was.
When asked why the ghost did it,
he had to admit it.
All he would say was "because."

So on the spider went
with a wondering intent
as to why the ghost chose her.
Over the flowers
the spider walked for hours
with the ghost as a passenger.

So then the spider
and it's spectral rider
came across the spiders three.
The arachnids made fun
of their brethren one
so off again they would be.

They never quit
kept on walking it—
into the distance they went.
Never finding acceptance—
they haven't been seen since,
as forced away they were sent.

pear head man
and bread boy

Nature did not have a plan
when it created
the Pear Head Man.
He had one friend
who was made of bread,
but the birdies ate him.
Now he's dead.

the alien ballerina

No one believes me
that I had seen a
happy dancing
alien ballerina.
It danced very badly
as though it were stiff.
It stopped dancing completely
after it went off the cliff.

the bunny came back

Billy had a bunny
that he loved very much.
He'd hug him, pet him
and squeeze him and such.

One day Billy awoke
to an awfully strange wiff
and ventured to find
that his bunny was stiff.

"Mommy! Mommy!" cried Billy.
"My bunny looks weird."
Billy's mother went to find their pet
exactly how she had feared.
In a box the bunny was put
for Billy to carry
and off they hurried
to the Pet Cemetary.

With sadness and tears,
the bunny was put into the ground.
Billy just stared quietly
at the buried bunny mound.

The very next morning
as dawn began to crack,
they opened the door
to find
the bunny came back.
All were speechless
as to what should be said—
how the bunny came back
even though it was dead.

No one could understand
how or why this could be—
but away they went back
and again buried that bunny.
Everyone stood there
just quietly nervous,
hoping and praying
this would be the last service.

the captain

A hole in the boat
made it no longer float
so into the sea it sank.
Luckily, a little island was found—
the captain wasn't to be drowned—
but on another problem he could bank.

devil bunny

A devil holding a bunny...
holding a devil...
holding a bunny...
holding a devil...
holding a bunny....
I'm so sorry
that this is
not funny.

the reindeer and the bumble bee

One of the weirdest things
that you could ever see
was a reindeer in love
with a bumble bee.
No one was sure how
or even remembered why—
how a creature that could walk
loved a creature that could fly.

To consumate this love,
they decided to kiss.
Unfortunately for them,
the bee did miss.
An accidental sting ripped out
what the bee had inside.
Without her innards,
she shortly there died.

Strucken with grief,
the reindeer then sobbed.
Devastated,
his heart had been robbed.
Sadly
this was not to be the worst of things.
It turned out
he was allergic to bee stings.

Clutching his chest,
he let out his final breath,
turned a strange colour...
then succumbed to death.
The akward day came—
no one knew what to do.
The proceedings were silent
as they buried the two.

weird family
weird baby

It's not a question
of maybe—
A weird family
makes a weird baby.

fly paper

A pleasant scent
beckoned me,
but I didn't know
it was so sticky.
I just cannot
fly or get free,
so now misery loves
a little company.

dance
of the
bedbugs

There once was a bear
named Popple fubbie.
He had a special pillow
that he called his "wubbie".
Late one nite,
Popple was very tired—
the thought of sleep
he admired.
So on went his jammies,
and he grabbed his bunny,
flicked on his light—
but something was funny.

BED BUGS

A dozen tiny bugs
danced on his bed.
Happy to see him—
bedbugs to be fed.
"Oh no!," exclaimed Popple.
"I can't sleep here.
You bugs eating me,
I surely do fear."
Looking around at all the bugs
in their places,
a thought of fear
could be seen on their faces.
As Popple turned to leave,
his bed he would not be sleeping.
He heard a weird sound—
a baby bedbug was weeping.

"Why do you cry,
tiny bug on my sheets?"
"I don't want to starve,"
said the bug.
"You were my only eats."
"I'm really sorry little bug
if it seems selfish of me—
but if you eat me,
I will no longer be
alive to do all the things that I please."
"We beg you," cried the bugs,
now sadly on their knees.
"I'll just sleep in another room,"
and away turned the bear.
"Oh, after you're sleeping,
we'll just eat you in there."

Suddenly Popple realized
the trouble he was in.
He couldn't go to sleep
without becoming din—din.
He played lots of loud music
and coffee he drank,
but slowly into
subconsiousness he sank.
Popple held his eyes open—
his life he must keep.
The bedbugs began yawning,
trying to trick himto sleep.
He fought as long as he could
before he began to topple—
but in the end,
the bugs had a bowl full of Popple.

boodini
and choobie

Boodini and Choobie—
what a magical pair.
A rotting magician...
a decomposing hare...
a trick gone wrong...
an illusion gone awry....
Their very last trick
was refusing to die.

the guy with a thing On his head-

There's not a whole lot
that can be said
for the poor guy
with a thing on his head.

eddie poe

Long ago
lived Eddie Poe,
in love with pumpkins
more than he should be.
Everyday he would visit.
If not, he would miss it.
Eddie would be a pumpkin
if he could be.

He didn't go away.
Instead he did stay
and fell asleep
in the pumpkin patch.
When he awoke,
nature played a joke.
Now he and the pumpkins
did match.

Someone took him
that day
who loved pumpkins
in a different way—
and made him into a yummy pie.
After this you see
you have to agree
what a horrible way for Eddie to die.

Hey!

Guess what boys and girls!
Many drawings in this book have little piggies hidden somewhere among them.
Why? I don't know.
I also don't think that this shirt is funny.

MR. PORKCHOP

about the author

An illustrator for numerous "underground" magazines Roman Dirge created his best know character, Lenore in 1992. The adventures of the cute little dead girl were seen in mini-comics and various magazines for several years afterward.

After running into Tim Burton at Solomon's garage in Los Angeles, Roman showed him his artwork. Mr. Burton describe his style as "beautiful" and "timeless."

This was encouraging.

After toying around working as a magician and a make up artist for several years, Roman decided to take the plunge and do "Lenore" as a full comic book series. "Lenore" became an instant cult success and launched Roman into other artistic endevours such as character design for TV animation and illustrating children's books. Currently, Roman resides in California where he loves tattoos, video games, martial arts, magic tricks and writing about himself in the third person.

Dirge007@Aol.Com
www.Spookyland.com

Printed in Canada